Servant
Leaders

A Pro   ONS

CRC Publications
Grand Rapids, Michigan

Servant Leaders: A Practical Guide for Deacons, © 2000 by CRC Publications, 2850 Kalamazoo Ave. SE, Grand Rapids, MI 49560. All rights reserved. With the exception of brief excerpts for review purposes, no part of this book may be reproduced in any manner whatsoever without written permission from CRC Publications. Printed in the United States of America on recycled paper. ⊕

We welcome your comments. Call us at 1-800-333-8300 or e-mail us at editors@crcpublications.org.

Library of Congress Cataloging-in-Publication Data
Vandezande, Ben, 1947-
    Servant leaders: a practical guide for deacons / Ben Vandezande.
        p. cm.
    Includes bibliographical references.
    ISBN -56212-773-X
    1. Deacons—Christian Reformed Church. I. Title.
    BX6826.V36 2000
    253'.088'257—dc21

                                                                    00-057162

10 9 8 7 6 5 4 3 2 1

Contents

How to Use This Guide

Congratulations! You've been called to serve as a deacon. Think of this guide as a toolkit to equip you for your calling. It will help you figure out what you're supposed to do and how to do it. As with any tool, the suggestions in this book won't do any good if you don't use them. They're meant to help you take on the hands-on tasks of diaconal ministry.

This guide is meant to be used as part of an orientation program for new deacons. It's divided into four parts, each containing a number of readings that introduce the topic, a discussion guide, and some notes for the discussion leader. Although this book is primarily directed at new deacons, experienced deacons will also be an important part of your group. Ideally each new deacon will be paired with a mentor or "buddy"—an experienced deacon who can help sort through the practical issues you'll face.

Here are two suggestions for using this guide in a group setting:

- Use the first part of four diaconal meetings to cover the four sections together. An experienced deacon can serve as a discussion leader. This person is not expected to know it all—her task is simply to keep the discussion on track. (You'll find notes for the discussion leader included at the end of each section.)
- Hold two to four orientation sessions for new deacons. Again, an experienced deacon should serve as discussion leader. You'll want to allow thirty to forty minutes for discussing each section.

How Do I Use These Tools?

- **Read.** Each of the four sections begins with some introductory reading. Take time to read these before each meeting.
- **Discuss.** Meet together with other new deacons or with the whole diaconate. Talk over the discussion questions at the end of each section. This will give you some practical insights on how to put your knowledge to work.
- **Connect.** Don't be tempted to skip this step! Newly elected deacons should be connected with a mentor—an experienced deacon who will help them answer the practical questions that will come up in their work. Take some time to share and pray with each other. Go out on visits together and reflect on those visits. New deacons who are connected to an experienced deacon will be ready to do ministry much sooner than those who are left to discover their task by themselves.

A Word to the Leader

Thank you for your willingness to walk alongside the newly elected deacons at your church in order to help them experience the joys of ministry. Please don't feel like you need to have all the answers. You're qualified to lead if you

- have a passion and enthusiasm for the ministry of the deacons.
- enjoy sharing your experiences with people.
- are willing to listen and provide guidance as requested.
- know about the ministries in your community and denomination.

In simple terms, your task is to help launch your church's newly elected deacons into this exciting ministry. As discussion leader, you'll lead the discussion of each section of this book, either with all the deacons or with the newly elected deacon(s) in your church. Along with the other experienced deacons in your church, you'll also serve as a "buddy" or mentor for a new deacon. This involves

- accompanying the deacon on visits.
- reflecting on your experiences together.
- praying for each other.

Ideally, each new deacon will be assigned a buddy deacon. If necessary, experienced deacons may serve as a mentor to more than one new deacon.

Each of the four sections in this book includes a discussion guide. At the end of each chapter, you'll find further notes addressed to you, the discussion leader.

Here are a few reminders you may find helpful as you use this material:

- Make sure each newly elected deacon has a copy of this guide.
- Let deacons know it is essential for each person to do the reading before meeting together for the discussion.
- Don't talk too much. While it may be tempting to go on at great length about any given topic, try to limit your talking time at any point to a couple of minutes. Then shift the focus to the newly elected deacons and ask a question of clarification or the next question in the discussion outline. This is especially important if your group is the whole diaconate. Remember, this is primarily for newer deacons.
- Don't let the discussion drag on. Keep it manageable and within the time frame. You can always follow up on some of these issues at a later time.

PART 1

The Calling and Tasks of the Deacon

As a deacon, you have been given the marvelous calling of engaging in the ministry of mercy and compassion on behalf of Jesus Christ. On these pages, you will find some descriptions of what it is that God calls you to do as a deacon. You won't find a detailed job description in the Bible, but the form for ordination and the church order of your denomination are both very helpful places to begin.

The God who calls you to serve as a deacon will also equip you to do your calling. God has gifted you in a special way to help others. You may be good at visiting. You may enjoy helping people with their finances. You may have a real passion for outreach. Perhaps your gift is in working with the poor in your community. Take some time to find your gift as a deacon and focus on that gift. Remember, *you do not have to be good at everything* deacons are called to do.

If you read over your denomination's form for the ordination of deacons, you will quickly realize that there is more work than any one person could do. That is why you are part of a team of deacons. You are not in this work alone. You have partners in ministry:

- Your fellow deacons each have gifts and experiences that can help you.
- Your family can be a tremendous source of support.
- The elders and pastor are your partners in this work.
- The congregation can help you carry out your calling.

The Charge to the Deacons

The following excerpts come from the form for Ordination of Elders and Deacons of the Christian Reformed Church in North America. Note that the actions a deacon is called to do are in **bold** type.

I charge you, deacons, to **inspire faithful stewardship** in this congregation. **Remind us** that "from everyone who has been given much, much will be demanded" (Luke 12:48). **Teach us** to be merciful. **Prompt us** to seize new opportunities to worship God with offerings of wealth, time and ability. **Realize** that benevolence is a quality of our life in Christ and not merely a matter of financial assistance. Therefore, **minister to rich**

7

and poor alike, both within and outside the church. **Weigh the needs of causes** and **use the church's resources** discerningly. **Be compassionate** to the needy. **Encourage** them with words that create hope in their hearts and with deeds that bring joy into their lives. **Be prophetic critics** of the waste, injustice, and selfishness in our society, and **be sensitive counselors** to the victims of such evils. **Let your lives be above reproach; live as examples of Christ Jesus; look to the interests of others.**

The Living Deacon

This exercise can help you "unpack" the calling of a deacon. The parts of the body can be a helpful reminder of what a deacon is called to do. Describe how each body part can help you carry out your work as a deacon. The first one is done for you.

Ears: listen to other people and understand them.

Eyes: _____.

Mouth: _____.

Heart: _____.

Hands: _____.

Arms: _____.

Knees: _____.

Feet: _____.

The Calling of the Deacon

As we've already seen from the form for ordination, deacons are charged with carrying out various forms of ministry. We'll look at these areas of ministry and what they involve, based on statements taken from the form for ordination and the Church Order of the Christian Reformed Church.

Note: If you are from another denomination, you may want to check your own forms and church order and compare the duties and responsibilities of deacons with the ones below.

1. Show mercy, encourage the needy
- Administer the mercy of Christ to all people.
- Help the congregation realize that benevolence is a quality of our life in Christ and not merely a matter of financial assistance.
- Show compassion to the needy and encourage them with words that bring hope and deeds that bring joy into their lives.
- Work using words of biblical encouragement and testimony that assure the unity of word and deed.

2. Inspire faithful stewardship, weigh the needs of causes
- Inspire faithful stewardship in the congregation.
- Remind the congregation that "from everyone who has been given much, much will be demanded" (Luke 12:48).
- Weigh the needs of causes and use the church's resources discerningly.
- Collect and disburse resources for benevolence.

3. Prompt congregational involvement
- Prompt the congregation to seize new opportunities to worship God with offerings of wealth, time, and ability.
- Teach the congregation to be merciful.

4. Minister to the poor
- Minister to rich and poor alike, both within and outside the church.
- Be compassionate to the needy.
- Be prophetic critics of waste, injustice, and selfishness in our society.
- Be sensitive counselors to the victims of such evils.
- Seek to cooperate with agencies in the community that are caring for the needy so that gifts may be distributed properly.
- Stimulate relief in Christ's name for the poor, distressed, and victims of injustice.
- Assess needs and develop programs of assistance.
- Demonstrate the care of the Lord in word as well as in deed.

5. Work with partners
- Cooperate with diaconates of neighboring churches.
- Enable the needy to make use of Christian institutions of mercy.
- Classes (regional church assemblies) shall assist the churches in their ministry of mercy. To administer this task each classis shall have a classis diaconal committee.
- Synod (governing body of the denomination) shall appoint a diaconal committee to administer the denominational ministry of mercy.

6. Provide leadership and accountability
- Every church shall have a council composed of ministers, elders, and deacons.
- The diaconate (deacons of the church) shall give an account of its work to the council.
- Deacons are to be Christlike and mature in faith. They are to exercise their office with prayer, patience, and humility.

Wanted: A Committed Deacon

So far we have explored the calling of deacons and the kinds of needs to which deacons respond in Christ's name. Christ wants to use us to do God's work. A humbling thought, but it's true. We work on Christ's behalf.

As a deacon, you need to

- **make a commitment** to spend a certain amount of time and energy each week, not only for meetings, but also for ministry. Set a minimum and a maximum amount of time you will set aside per week.
- **work within the gifts** with which the Lord has blessed you. Focus your work. Take the time to develop your gifts through study and training.
- **keep a balance** between your work, family life, and church work. If you're married, involve your spouse as a partner in your work.
- **renew yourself spiritually** on a regular basis. Pray a lot—individually and as a diaconate. Celebrate what God does through you.

You also need to be part of a team—together with the other deacons, you form the diaconate. The diaconate works best when the members

- provide support to one another and create a safe place to share experiences and pray together.
- have a clear, written work plan that describes who does what. This provides accountability, establishes a common purpose, provides a focus, enables deacons to evaluate what is being done, and offers a sense of accomplishment.

A Sample Work Plan

On page 11 is a sample work plan for one diaconate. Notice that the contact deacon takes the lead in this area of ministry, but that doesn't mean he does it alone. Other deacons are still involved. Take a few minutes to look over the work plan.

Areas of Ministry	Activities	Contact Deacon	Partners in ministry
1. Show mercy, encourage the needy	1. Visit the elderly (75+) 2x/year	Bill	
	2. Visit shut-ins 4x/year	Bill	Care callers in district
	3. Tape ministry - those sick/shut in	Bill	Fred/tape; Ineke/bring
	4. Big brother to single parent children	Dick	2 young adults
	5. Financial help - emergency	All	Deacons in District
	6. Tuition assistance (4 families)	Tom	
	7. Problem solve: 2 long term cases	All	Partners in the congregation meet each month
2. Inspire faithful stewardship, weigh the needs of causes	1. Promote offerings each Sunday	Tom	Stewardship committee
	2. Prepare offering schedule	Tom	+ chair, + exec of council
	3. Deal with requests as they come	Tom	
	4. Educate about wills	John	+ CSS; stewardship committee
3. Prompt congregation involvement	1. Recruit counting committee	Tom	5 people count money
	2. Contact with care coordinators	All	In each district
	3. Recruit volunteers for community agency	Susan	Recruit 7 people
	4. Promote deacon service opportunities	John	Newsletter - "Deacon's bench"
4. Minister to the poor	1. Respond to food calls	John	Assign to response teams
	2. Collect for food bank: 12 x/year	Dick	Young adults promote/deliver
	3. Gather clothes for pregnancy centre	Susan	Young couples club
	4. Follow up contacts	Dick	Long term partners
	5. Sponsor young people on SERVE	Susan	6 young people for one week
	6. Serve on Neighbourlink board	Susan	Committee of 4
5. Work with partners	1. Attend new deacon/chair workshop	All	Send a representative to board
	2. Spring diaconal conference	All	
	3. Contact with Home for Aged	Bill	Invite elders/caregivers
	4. Promote community development	Dick	
	5. Promote CRWRC (world relief) in the congregation	Dick	CRWRC contact person
	6. Promote CRWRC offerings	Tom	Stewardship committee
6. Provide leadership: a) council (reporting) b) committees	1. Report to council	John	
	2. Serve on executive committee	John	
	3. Serve on stewardship committee	Tom	+ stewardship committee
	4. Prepare minutes	Dick	
Be accountable: a) deacon's meetings b) study c) mutual support	1. Meet monthly	All	
	2. Study	All	
	3. Buddy system	Pairs	
	4. Pray for needy	All	+ prayer partners

Discussion Guide

1. Check In

Take a few minutes to greet and touch base with each other. After the leader or someone from the group opens with prayer, think about the following questions. Be prepared to share your answers briefly.

- How did you feel on the day you were elected?
- What do you most want to learn to help you in being a deacon?

2. Characteristics of a Deacon

Read 1 Timothy 3:8-10, which describes the person of the deacon.

- Name the main characteristics of a deacon.
- Why are these important for a deacon to have?

3. Tasks of the Deacon

Review the charge to the deacons.

- What strikes you as you look at the charge to the deacons?
- Review the "Living Deacon" exercise. Share your thoughts with the group.

4. Develop a Clear Focus

If you asked most people what a deacon does, they'd probably come up with one or more of the following ideas: deacons are in charge of Sunday offerings, they help a few people in financial need, they collect food, and they support denominational world relief efforts. But even a quick reading of the charge to deacons points us to a broader vision of a deacon's calling. It is important for you as a deacon to get a clear focus of your calling. That will enable you to have a clear sense of purpose and of your identity as a deacon.

- In your own words, what is the purpose of a deacon?
- If deacons really performed all the activities described in the charge to deacons, what do you think God would accomplish through them?

5. A Job Description

Take a moment to review the sample work plan on page 11.

- How would such a work plan help you as a deacon?
- How would "contact deacons" help you focus your work?
- Note the examples of how this diaconate involves the congregation in its work. What are the advantages to this kind of involvement?
- Ask the discussion leader to share what your local diaconate is doing. Go over the work plan of the diaconate if one is available.
- Discuss with each other what is expected of deacons in your church in each of the following areas:
  —council meetings
  —deacon meetings
  —taking the offering
  —care groups or households of faith
  —ministry in the community

Don't forget to prepare for the next session by reading "Part 2: The Visiting Deacon."

Leaders

Introduction

As you begin this first session, take a moment to explain your role. Explain that you are a deacon who is eager to share from your experience and help others discover the joy of being a deacon. You are not the authority. Stress that this is a time of mutual learning.

1. Check In

Open the meeting with prayer, or ask one of the deacons to do so. Then ask deacons to briefly identify how they felt when they were elected and what they would most like to learn in these discussions.

2. Characteristics of a Deacon

Ask someone to look up and read 1 Timothy 3:8-10. Then discuss the characteristics of a deacon and why these characteristics are important for deacons to have.

3. Tasks of a Deacon

Ask someone to read the charge to deacons out loud. Then ask the group to respond to the discussion question "What strikes you as you look at the charge to the deacons?" Review participants' answers to the "Living Deacon" exercise.

4. Develop a Clear Focus

Be ready to share what you understand to be the purpose of a deacon in a sentence or two.

5. A Job Description

If your diaconate has a job description, a work plan, or a list of activities, please bring copies along. Be prepared to share it with the deacons. Take some time to walk through the job description and what is expected of the deacon at the local level on a one-to-one basis.

PART 2

The Visiting Deacon

When you visit people in your congregation or community, you are bringing hope in Jesus' name. In this section, you will read and talk about some practical tips for making visits. Remember that there's no substitute for actually going out on some visits with an experienced deacon. After your visit, talk it over together.

A "must-read" for all deacons is the book *90% of Helping Is Just Showing Up* (CRC Publications, 1-800-333-8300). Author James R. Kok argues that intimacy, not answers, is what people need most. As a deacon, you need to simply be present in people's lives and let God lead them (and you) into the next steps. Don't wait until you feel like some kind of "expert" before you visit people. Just show up, listen, and share.

Go with God!

Visiting people is the heart of a deacon's work. Deacons visit as representatives of God, the "Father of our Lord Jesus Christ, the Father of compassion and the God of all comfort, who comforts us in all our troubles, so that we can comfort those in any trouble with the comfort we ourselves have received" (2 Cor. 1:3-4). They serve as a channel of Christ's love and concern.

You can be agents of mercy only because you yourselves have experienced the mercy, compassion, and encouragement of God. Your visits are not so much about what you do as what God does through you.

Six Strategies for an Effective Visit

These strategies will help you to be a vehicle for God's comfort and love.

1. Wrap your visit in prayer. Pray before you go; ask God to guide you. Share your uncertainties with God.
2. Listen! Listen! Listen! Come to listen and hear the person you're visiting. Don't come to "fix" something. Listen well and communicate your love and acceptance. Be in touch with yourself.
3. Know what you're good at and focus there. Don't be afraid to say "I don't know" if you don't.

4. Ensure confidentiality. The biggest gift you have to offer during your visit is that the person's story is safe with you. Always ask permission before you share anyone's story.

5. Point beyond yourself to God. You can do this by offering words of encouragement, a brief word from Scripture, and prayer.

6. If you try problem solving, listen well to the need and clarify what you hear; define the problem together; together plan how to resolve it.

Who Should a Deacon Visit?

Look over the following list. Check the people on this list you think a deacon should visit.

_____ 1. a shut-in who has crippling arthritis
_____ 2. those who have long-term illnesses
_____ 3. someone without appropriate housing
_____ 4. a church member who can't make ends meet
_____ 5. an unemployed person in your neighborhood
_____ 6. a family struggling to meet Christian school tuition payments
_____ 7. a person who feels lonely and left out in the church
_____ 8. an elderly person in the community whose children never visit
_____ 9. a widow grieving the loss of her husband
_____ 10. a couple who have just had their first baby
_____ 11. a senior on his eightieth birthday
_____ 12. a single parent having a tough time
_____ 13. a child who has run away from home
_____ 14. a person who has been abused
_____ 15. a family on welfare trying to find work and make a new start
_____ 16. an alcoholic looking for help
_____ 17. a couple who overspends and needs to learn budgeting
_____ 18. a single parent facing a crisis pregnancy

Learn How to Listen

Listening is a gift you can give. It creates an atmosphere of trust and acceptance with the one you are listening to. Your gift of listening helps people put their thoughts and feelings into words, which is their first step toward helping themselves.

Listening also helps people build relationships with each other and God. If we listen carefully, we can explore a variety of needs. And we will know what to pray when the time comes.

We'll use the following case study about Susan to learn some effective strategies for listening. As you read, imagine that Susan is a member of your church, and you are going to be her deacon. Imagine that you are about to meet with Susan. Think about some possible needs to listen for during your visit.

Susan is a thirty-six-year-old single parent of three children (David, thirteen; Sam, ten; Jane, eight). She divorced her husband three years ago after several years of neglect and abuse. Just after the divorce, Susan transferred her membership to Grace Church. Last fall she went back to school to train as a bookkeeper. Although Susan started attending the women's Bible study group two years ago, she has been absent a lot lately. Because of the pressure of raising the children as a single parent, running the home, and doing schoolwork, she finds any other activity hard to fit in. She is often quite lonely. She has not made many friends, except for a few women in the Bible study.

Susan's ex-husband lives in a community a half-hour away. He pays child support (set at $100 per week) only occasionally. Susan receives supplemental assistance from the government. Her family lives forty-five minutes away and is not very involved with her. They are not convinced that she should have gone through with the divorce.

Two Kinds of Questions
One way to understand a person is by asking questions. Try asking open-ended questions that encourage longer answers instead of questions that can be answered with a yes or no.

Closed: Are you tired at the end of the day, Susan?

Open: How do you feel after a busy day?

For Reflection

What is the difference between these two ways of asking questions?

Reflect Content and Feelings
Reflecting means listening to understand what others say. In order to better understand a statement, we repeat the statement in our own words, thus giving the other person a chance to clarify or expand on her thoughts and feelings.

Here are some examples of reflecting content:

Susan: No one comes to see me anymore.

Deacon: You haven't had a lot of visitors lately.

Susan: No I haven't. I wish I could see some of the women from my Bible study once in a while.

Deacon: You wish some of your friends would come.

Here are some examples of reflecting feelings:

Susan: No one comes to see me anymore.

Deacon: It sounds like you feel lonely.

Susan: Yes I am. I see some people in my bookkeeping class but it isn't the same. I used to love going out. But now I'm stuck at home.

Deacon: It seems like that makes you feel sad.

For Reflection

Why is it important to reflect feelings as well as content?

Listen for Understanding
This conversation between Susan and her deacon takes place in a restaurant over lunch. The first few minutes are spent talking about the restaurant, the weather, and what to order.

Susan:	I don't go out for lunch much.
Deacon:	I guess that's hard to get around to in your busy life.
Susan:	I can't really afford it…. Sometimes I go out with the kids on their birthday. That way they have something special.
Deacon:	Do you get a chance to go out with your parents and your family?
Susan:	Not really. We don't talk much since the divorce. They were pretty against it, you know. I go to family get-togethers. But I always feel like I'm the black sheep … and I guess I am.
Deacon:	It sounds like you feel abandoned.
Susan:	Sometimes. But I can't let it bother me. I'm too busy. By the time I get home from school, make supper, run a load of laundry, clean up, help the kids with papers, do homework, drive them to sports … it's hard to find the energy. It's hardest late at night.
Deacon:	What kind of thoughts come to you then?
Susan:	The kids. I worry about them. We've just moved for the second time in five years. I needed to do it in order to get away from Tom and be close enough to school, but I'm concerned about the effect all of this is having on my children.
Deacon:	All of the moving is hard on them.
Susan:	Yes, it is. They had to change schools in the middle of the year, and they have a hard time making new friends. Steven is in junior high and friends are very important to him. He's really angry with me about this.
Deacon:	How does that leave you feeling?
Susan:	Oh, I just wish I could make everyone happy…. But my kids are hurting and there's not much I can do about it. I can't stop thinking about it. Every time I see Steven feeling upset I feel worse.
Deacon:	This situation seems to be really eating at you.

For Reflection

1. How could you tell the deacon was really paying attention in the conversation?
2. In their conversation, find an example of
   • an open-ended question
   • reflecting content
   • reflecting feelings

Listen to Explore Needs

After their lunch conversation, the deacon invites Susan and the kids over for a picnic with several other families. Since Susan had mentioned her financial struggles during their previous conversation, the deacon asks her to jot down her income and expenses so they can discuss her finances in more detail during their next visit. The following is part of their conversation during a visit three weeks later.

Deacon:	Last time you mentioned that your ex-husband is supposed to send child support of $100 per month, but he doesn't always do it. Doesn't that mean your finances are pretty tight sometimes?
Susan:	It's worst on special days and when school starts. There is just nothing left over.
Deacon:	I would think that finances create a lot of pressure for you. One thing we do as deacons on behalf of the church is pitch in to help. Maybe you could use some help with—
Susan:	[interrupts] I don't know. I don't want everyone to know I'm getting help.

Deacon:	I can appreciate that. That's why we don't tell anyone. This information is strictly confidential … only the deacons know.
Susan:	*[hesitantly]* Oh …
Deacon:	Does that help?
Susan:	Yes … but I'm still not sure I need the help.
Deacon:	Why don't we begin by looking at some of those numbers?
Susan:	Oh yeah. I have it right here. *[She pulls a sheet of paper out of her purse and goes over her basic income and expenses. It shows that she just breaks even.]*
Deacon:	Boy, that's a tight squeeze. How do you manage when the car breaks down or when your ex-husband doesn't come through?
Susan:	I don't. *[laughs]* Listen to me, here I am laughing about it. Usually I get upset. Sometimes I babysit or get a part time job doing books. I juggle a lot.
Deacon:	Do you feel that you need a regular amount each month in order to help you break even?

For Reflection

How did the deacon help Susan feel more comfortable about sharing her financial needs?

How to Build Prayer into a Visit

Our visits need to be wrapped in prayer—not to make the visit "Christian" but because we need to bring the person's needs and our own needs before God. Building prayer into our visits occurs naturally when we focus on listening and understanding needs. Notice in the following example that Susan's deacon doesn't simply pray *for* her; instead the deacon helps bring her specific needs before God. The prayer grows out of the understanding that develops throughout the visit.

The following conversation takes place after Susan and her deacon have discussed her finances and her struggles as a single parent.

Deacon:	I really appreciate your willingness to share with me. I've learned a lot and yet I feel like I still have a lot to learn. You need a lot of wisdom and strength in your situation. I want you to know I'll pray for you.
Susan:	I sure could use it sometimes.
Deacon:	Would you appreciate a time of prayer right now? *[pause]* We've talked about lots of feelings and some struggles. Would you like to share these with God in prayer?
Susan:	Sure, I guess so.
Deacon:	In my prayer I would like to ask God to keep you close and provide you with wisdom. Is there anything else you'd like us to pray about?
Susan:	How to deal with my son's anger … and I just want some friends to visit with.
Deacon:	We'll invite God to help you with your son's anger. Let's ask God to lead you to a friend or two. And I'd like to pray that the children would feel at home soon.
Susan:	That would be good.
Deacon:	OK, let's pray…. *[the deacon offers a brief prayer based on Susan's input]*

For Reflection

How did the deacon effectively build prayer into the visit with Susan?

When to Pray

- Prayer should be a natural part of a visit. Because prayer cannot be programmed beforehand, you'll need to determine the proper moment to pray during each visit. That judgment depends on the person's needs, not yours. In other words, pray when you sense that the person you're visiting is ready, not when you are ready. Careful listening will help you ascertain when prayer is appropriate. Let prayer be a natural part of your conversation, not an intrusion or interruption.
- Don't artificially tack prayer onto a visit. Prayer is not a vehicle for introducing your Christian viewpoint. The entire visit is an opportunity to demonstrate your love and concern. If that doesn't shine through the rest of the conversation, prayer will not "make it Christian."
- Although it is common practice to close a visit with prayer, consider occasionally praying with people at other times during the visit. Prayer is not a technique for closing a visit. If you always close with prayer, the people you're visiting might come to look on the prayer as a way to say goodbye rather than a way to communicate with God. They may even feel disappointment when you mention prayer, because it signals that you will be leaving. Remember that prayer can come appropriately at any time during a visit.
- Avoid the temptation of using prayer as a means to manipulate. For example, praying, "Heavenly Father, I come before you today asking that you would bring about a change of heart in Mary, so that she would become willing to join the choir," is merely an attempt to force Mary's hand by arousing feelings of guilt. A prayer of this sort will have negative results. If, on the other hand, Mary expresses a desire to pray for a change of heart, such a prayer could be appropriate. In that case the prayer is coming from Mary's expressed needs, not your own agenda.

How to Pray

Introducing the Prayer

Initiating prayer is awkward for some people. What do you say when you sense that prayer is appropriate? If you want to avoid the simple declaration "Let us pray," try one of the following:

- "Would you appreciate a prayer right now?"
- "We have talked about this problem and you have expressed a lot of feelings. Would you like to share these with God in prayer?"
- "You have set a personal goal for yourself. Would you like to ask God for help?"
- "I'm really glad things have gone well with you this week. Shall we share our thanks with God in prayer?"

These introductions leave the individual with a choice. Prayer needs to be a willing response.

When Someone Says No

Much of the time, when you ask people if they would like to pray, your suggestion will be welcome. Of course, they may also say no. On those occasions, many people will offer a reason. Whatever the reason, you need not become defensive or think that you are being rejected. Remember that as your relationship develops there might be other occasions when the person will feel more open to prayer. Be patient!

What to Pray About

Pray about the need that suggested prayer in the first place. This will enable you to focus the prayer, which will also make it more meaningful for the other person. Both of you will benefit if you are clear about the needs you will bring to God before you pray. The following example shows how to ensure that both of you understand which needs will be included in prayer.

> Mrs. Thompson is facing surgery the next morning. She tells you she is worried and afraid. By asking open-ended questions, you encourage Mrs. Thompson to express her real concerns. After listening to her, you ask if she would like to pray, and she says yes. Your conversation might go something like this:
>
> *Deacon:* Before we pray, what are some of your thoughts and feelings right now?
>
> *Mrs. T:* I'm worried that after surgery is over, I won't be able to take care of my children. I feel so alone right now.
>
> *Deacon:* You'd like us to pray about your fears of loneliness and your worries that something might happen tomorrow that would prevent you from being a good mother to your children?
>
> *Mrs. T:* Yes. I know I shouldn't feel this way and think these thoughts, but what if I die?
>
> *Deacon:* It sounds as if we should ask God to help you as you struggle with this fear of death. Is there anything else you would like to share with God in prayer?
>
> *Mrs. T:* No, these are my chief concerns.

By inviting Mrs. Thompson to share her concerns, you have information to use in building a prayer that meets her needs.

When Someone Asks You to Pray

Occasionally someone will request a prayer. When that happens, you might be tempted to immediately fold your hands and begin praying. But remember that prayer should meet the person's needs. A good response includes finding out more about the person's need. You might say something like this: "I would be glad to pray with you. But before I do, I'd like you to share with me what you're thinking and what your needs are at this time. That way we can share them better with God." The point is not to stall but to provide better quality ministry.

Share Words of Hope

Deacons are invited to "encourage people with words that bring hope and deeds that bring joy into their lives." Can you think of words that bring hope to people?

Sometimes it's hard to know what to say. Sometimes it's best to say nothing and simply be with a person.

Words That Refresh

"May the Lord show mercy to the household of Onesiphorus, because he often refreshed me and was not ashamed of my chains" (2 Tim. 1:16). Paul honors Onesiphorus as one who stood by him in prison.

The word "refresh" in the Bible has several meanings—physical refreshment, encouragement, and spiritual renewal. That kind of refreshment comes from deeds *and* words.

Deacons are encouragers too. During your visits you will find yourself needing to share a word of encouragement in a variety of situations.

- A young couple who are trying to make ends meet need a word of encouragement to stick with a budget plan.
- A single parent needs a word of encouragement as he tries to cope with the demands of raising of his two children.
- A widow needs to be encouraged to grieve the loss of her husband and lay that grief before the Lord.
- An unemployed person needs words of encouragement as she looks for new work but is constantly faced with closed doors.

Speak God's Word

As a deacon, you have an inexhaustible resource for bringing words of hope. But only when you draw from the riches of the Bible yourself will you be able to speak God's word of comfort to others. For that reason it's important to spend time in prayer and meditation of God's Word *before* you go on a visit.

Choose a psalm to reflect on—perhaps Psalm 23 or Psalm 62. These speak of God's leading and of how God can help us find peace in the midst of turmoil. Immerse yourself in the words before you go on a visit.

While you are there, listen with all of your heart. Listen for content and feelings. Pay attention to expressions of being overwhelmed by grief. Invite the person to pour out her heart to God like the psalmist in Psalm 62.

Which Passage?

The more we immerse ourselves in God's Word, the more we will be able to share appropriate words of hope and comfort with others. A deacon's meeting is a great time to share helpful passages with each other.

Some deacons paste a list of favorite passages into the front of their pocket Bible or use Post-its to mark appropriate passages.

Here are some suggestions:

- Psalm 23; Hebrews 13:5-6. God will not forsake us in our time of pain.
- Psalm 61. Asking God to lift us out of our difficulty to a rock higher than we are.
- Psalm 62. Finding peace in the midst of turmoil.
- Psalm 63. The need for prayer.
- Psalm 90. Our hope is in God.

- Philippians 4:6-7; 1 Peter 5:7. Bring your anxieties to God, who cares for you.
- Romans 5:10-11; 1 John 1:9. Forgiveness is a gift and a promise.
- Galatians 4:5; Romans 8:15. God is our Father (Abba).
- 2 Corinthians 8:1-7; 9:6-7. The joy of giving generously to God.
- Galatians 6:9; Isaiah 41:10. Don't give up; God will strengthen you.
- Romans 8:1; Isaiah 1:18. There is no guilt too great for God.
- Romans 4:20-21; 1 John 5:14-15. Trust in God; claim God's promises.

What's Your Favorite Passage?

This is a good question to ask when you are on a visit. People often have in mind Bible passages that especially speak to them when they are struggling. Asking this question allows them to repeat God's own words of comfort. Also ask, "Why is this passage especially helpful to you?"

Ask the same questions of your fellow deacons, your family, your pastor, and so on. Let others share with you the passages that speak to them.

List two or three of your own favorite passages and write down why they are your favorite.

1. _____

2. _____

3. _____

What Can I Do to Help?

The following suggestions for caring for those who are sick are from Wendy Bergren, who died on February 12, 1985.

I am a married young woman struggling to beat cancer. My husband and I have three children: a baby, a preschooler, and a first grader. Since I am severely ill, we depend on our friends for survival. Over the months, so many of my friends have asked, "What can I do?" Here are some ideas.

- Cook a meal for my family, but offer a choice of two courses (because one week, we had tuna noodle casserole four nights in a row) and bring it in disposable containers or marked pots (because if I can't return your casserole, I cry at my powerlessness and confusion).
- Make your offer specific. Say, "I want to come over Monday at 3 o'clock to bake cookies or clean your pantry shelf." If you say, "Call me any time for anything," I don't know what you want to do or when you are free … so I probably won't ask.
- Offer to babysit—even if my husband and I stay home. This gives us the freedom of a private adult life in a place my illness can cope with.
- Help with holidays, birthdays, and anniversaries. Ask if there are any special gifts or cards or wrapping papers you could pick up for me. How many times I have wanted to give my husband a special thank-you card or put up a holiday decoration, but have been unable!
- Take snapshots of my children over the months. This gives me a feeling that there are permanent records of the temporary happenings I must miss.

- Allow me to feel sad or prepare for the worst. One of the most difficult problems of having a serious illness is that everyone wants to encourage me; but sometimes the luxury of having a good cry with a friend who will allow it lets the tension escape—once the dam has broken.
- Even if the joke is terrible, tell it! Share your humor. Bring *Reader's Digest* and read aloud. Describe what is funny out there. It may not tickle my ribs today, but tomorrow I may relish it! Speak to the part of me that is more alive than dead, for that is the real me.
- Touch me. The isolation of being an invalid makes the power of love even sweeter.
- Say the word *cancer* around me, and talk about the real life you are living. This helps me feel less like an untouchable and like I am still involved with the world. One of the hardest things about being an invalid is the problem of being isolated from what's going on. If you don't talk to me about life outside, I am left with only illness and TV to talk with my husband about, and this is hard.
- Encourage your husband to come over to visit my husband in the evenings. One of the greatest gifts I have is my husband, and yet my illness has eliminated many of his pleasures. How happy I am when I hear him laughing with a friend in his shop or cheering Monday night football with a pal!
- Pray for me and say so. The fact that you have faith gives me faith.

Discussion Guide

1. Check In
- Take a few minutes to touch base with each other and share what's going on in each other's lives.
- Afterward, take turns praying out loud for the person on your left. Pray for a blessing on that person as they learn to become a deacon.
- Read 2 Corinthians 1:3-5 as an introduction to the discussion on visiting.

2. The Heart of a Deacon's Work
- Review the section "Six Strategies for an Effective Visit."
- Were you surprised by any of the people on the list in the exercise "Who Should a Deacon Visit"?

3. Would You Ask for Help?
Let's face it. Most people don't call the diaconate for help. Why is that? Let's make it more personal. If you had a financial need or some other need—loneliness, sadness, sickness—would you call on the deacons for help?
- Why or why not?
- What would make you hesitate?
- Describe how you might feel if you had to ask for help.

4. Learn How to Listen
Discuss the following questions as you reflect on the conversation between the deacon and Susan in the section "Listen for Understanding."
- Why are open-ended questions helpful in this conversation?
- Why did the deacon offer the help to Susan?
- How can you effectively build prayer into a visit?

5. When You Visit the Sick
Review the section "What Can I Do to Help?" Imagine that you are a deacon who will visit with Wendy Bergren.
- What is the first thing that you should try to do?
- What are some of the needs of this family?
- What could the deacons and the congregation do to meet the family's needs?

6. Let's Go Visit!
Visiting is the heart of a deacon's work. In connecting with people one-on-one we share the mercy of Christ. With a partner, take some time in the next couple of months to visit people in your congregation and your community. Get a feeling for what is involved. After each visit, reflect with your partner about what happened, using the following questions.

- Did the visit go well? Why or why not?
- How did you arrange the visit?
- How did you prepare yourself?
- Did you offer words of encouragement? Did you build prayer into the visit? How and when?

Don't forget to prepare for the next session by reading "Part 3: Providing Long-term Help."

Leaders

1. Check In

After a time of sharing about what is going on in people's lives, ask each person to pray out loud for the person sitting on his or her left. This gives people a chance to practice praying for others as part of their ministry. The suggested Scripture passage (2 Cor. 1:3-5) is a great introduction to a discussion on visiting.

2. The Heart of a Deacon's Work

Take a moment to review the strategies for an effective visit. Then look at the exercise "Who Should a Deacon Visit?" Ask if the deacons were surprised by any of the names on the list of people a deacon should visit.

3. Would You Ask for Help?

The purpose of this exercise is to get deacons to reflect on the fact that in many cases we as deacons wouldn't ask for help ourselves. It's not an easy thing to do. Simply read the questions from the discussion guide and then pause to allow each person (including yourself) to respond.

4. Learn How to Listen

The conversation between Susan and her deacon ("Listen for Understanding") is intended to give new deacons a feel for how various listening skills can be used in a visit. Briefly touch on the three questions in the discussion outline.

5. When You Visit the Sick

The section "What Can I Do to Help?" should help deacons think through what they need to anticipate as they visit with someone who is sick. Help deacons recognize that (a) our first response should be to build a relationship; (b) a diversity of needs exist, not only for the person who is ill, but also for members of the family; (c) other people can be involved in meeting the needs.

6. Let's Go Visit!

The information in this section will come alive only when deacons go on visits together. Have each of the new deacons and their mentors plan a time when they can visit someone in the church and in the community. Deacons should use the questions in the Discussion Guide to reflect on each visit after it has been completed.

PART 3

Providing Long-term Help

"Give a person a fish and he will eat for a day; teach him to fish and he will eat for a lifetime." While this familiar proverb is often associated with missionary work overseas, its wisdom applies especially to the work of deacons locally.

In working with people over the long term, deacons are especially interested in affirming others' gifts and capacities. The goal is for people to increasingly use the gifts that God has given them and build on their strengths so that they can help themselves.

In this section we will focus on the role of deacons as helpers. We'll look at what happens after the initial visit and find out how to go beyond offering relief to encouraging and affirming people's own gifts and responsibilities. You'll find that the guidelines in this section apply whether you are working with members of your congregation or people in your community. In both cases, deacons are partners in ministry with those they serve.

A Quiz for Helpers

How do deacons provide help for the long term?

The form for ordination that we looked at in Part 1 says,

> Help us [the congregation] realize that benevolence is a quality of our life in Christ and not merely a matter of financial assistance.

The focus here is not on *what* we give, but *how* we give it.

Please answer the following questions as honestly as you can.

1. If you had a financial need, would you go to the deacons for help?
   ☐ Yes   ☐ No   ☐ If I were desperate   ☐ Other _____

2. If the deacons offered you financial help, how would you feel about receiving it?
   ☐ Great   ☐ Hesitant   ☐ Guilty   ☐ Other _____

3. Do you feel compassion toward those with financial need?
   ☐ Yes   ☐ No   ☐ Depends   ☐ Other _____

4. Can you accept someone after you see that they have made mistakes?
☐ Yes   ☐ No   ☐ It gets harder   ☐ Other _____

5. Do you understand that someone may have different priorities from your own?
☐ Yes   ☐ No   ☐ For a while   ☐ Other _____

6. Do you recognize when you can't help people because their priorities and values are just too different from your own?
☐ Yes   ☐ No   ☐ I would need help   ☐ Other _____

For Reflection

What strikes you as you look over your responses?

7. Do you look for skills and abilities in others and encourage them to use their gifts?
☐ Yes   ☐ No   ☐ Other _____

How Should We Help?

Visiting with people often involves helping them. But helping is not the same thing as "fixing" a problem *for* them.

- **Helping means allowing yourself to be used as an instrument of Christ's mercy and love.** Each person you visit is someone God calls you to respect, care for, and love.
- **Helping means journeying with people through their problem or crisis.** But before you can expect growth and change to take place, you need to accept where the person is now. Remember that you can accept the *person* without approving problematic behaviors. This means choosing to have a non-judgmental attitude toward the person.
- **Helping is finding ways to enable people** to
  —define their problem.
  —gain understanding and insight.
  —explore options.
  —choose a course of action.

The key to helping people over the long term is remembering that they have the ability and the inner resources to cope with and find solutions to their own problems. You cannot solve their problems for them.

Going Beyond Relief: A Case Study

Mrs. G has a physical disability and is on a pension. When she receives notice from the electric company that they will disconnect her service unless they receive payment in two days, she calls her pastor to request financial help.

The deacons who visit find the home quite run down. Mrs. G can't find the disconnect notice, but a call to the electric company confirms it. The company also states that the payment must be paid in full because of Mrs. G's record of nonpayment.

Mrs. G tells the deacons that there is no food in the house. Her eighteen-year-old daughter lives in the basement with her eleven-month-old grandson. The baby's playpen is in poor shape and is quite unsafe. The baby needs food and disposable diapers.

The daughter's boyfriend, who has been out of work for some time, also lives with Mrs. G. He and Mrs. G's daughter contribute only $50 a month for food. Mrs. G's former husband often moves in toward the end of the month when his welfare check runs out. He is sometimes abusive and does not contribute financially to the household.

Rounding out the home are the pets—a rather fierce dog and two or three cats. Neighbors call the Humane Society regularly to complain. These animals are Mrs. G's only source of affection.

The deacons decide to pay the balance of the electric bill. They also buy $45 worth of groceries for Mrs. G, as well as diapers and formula for the baby. They are able to locate a fairly new playpen from a family in the congregation.

Mrs. G is grateful to receive these items. While the daughter rummages through the groceries to see what's there, the boyfriend calls up the stairs, "Has your mom got food for us yet?"

As they turn to go, the deacons give Mrs. G their phone numbers. They wish her well and assure her that God cares for her.

The following month Mrs. G calls the deacons back again, asking for food to tide them over until the end of the month. How should the deacons respond?

For Reflection

1. What were the "presenting needs" in this situation? Did the deacons respond well to them?
2. How should the deacons respond to the second call for help?

Financial Needs: Examining Your Attitude

Deacons want to help others through difficult times materially and spiritually. At the same time, most people have personal feelings about financial assistance and how money should be used. In order for you to effectively help others, it's important for you to understand your own feelings about money.

- *Think about how it feels for members of your church to come to the deacons for help.* These members may not be "poor" compared to those who live in areas of the globe characterized by widespread poverty, but they may be in the midst of a financial crisis that makes them feel equally oppressed. Our North American culture is based on personal independence and affluence. Asking for help usually means the burden has become impossible to carry alone. Most of those who come to the deacons for help have already used all of their other resources, including family and friends. Asking the deacons for help is probably a last resource, taken when there seem to be no other options.
- *Acknowledge your own thoughts and feelings about people who need help from the church.* Ask yourself questions like these: Do I feel compassion in my heart toward those with financial needs? Can I refrain from judging people's abilities or faith because of their situation? Can I accept people after I see they have made mistakes? Can I show true respect for people simply as human beings

For Reflection

What's your attitude toward money? Does it control you? Does it comfort you? Does it make you feel secure?

made in God's image? Can I look for their skills and encourage them to use those skills? How can I share my faith and hope for the future with them?

- *Understand your own feelings about the use of money.* Each of us has a personal system of handling money and material purchases. Our budget reflects our personal priorities. As a deacon, understanding your personal priorities about the use of money and material goods is an important part of working with those who have financial needs. Ask yourself, Can I understand that others' priorities may differ from my own? Can I accept that a different priority system may be as valid as mine? Can I teach financial management skills without insisting on my own priorities? Will I know when to step aside because the priorities and values of the person I'm trying to help are just too different from my values?

Helping People with Financial Needs: A Step-by-Step Guide

The material in this section was prepared by Sherrie Kornoelje.

1. Take Time to Reflect

Before working with a family or individual, it's important to consider your personal attitude. Recognize that your attitude may vary, depending on what else is going on in your life. Try to clear your mind of personal issues that could affect your relationship with the people you are trying to help. Disregard any unfounded information you may have heard prior to meeting with them. Above all, be ready to let God work in and through you. Prepare yourself to listen openly and without judgment, thereby communicating God's loving care and compassion.

You should also prepare for the time you spend together.

- Plan your day to avoid having to rush before or during your visit.
- Set aside a quiet time before your visit.
- Pray for the Holy Spirit's presence in the visit.
- Pray for an open heart and the ability to listen as you focus on the family's need.
- Meditate on Scripture that focuses on the all-encompassing love of Jesus.

2. Assess the Situation

Your initial visits will give you an opportunity to assess the situation. Your assessment will focus on three main areas: (1) defining the problem and identifying abilities, (2) considering options for solutions, and (3) making a choice. Keep in mind these general rules when assessing the financial needs of others:

- Every family is unique and needs to be treated with dignity and respect. We cannot use one strategy to help everyone. Individual responses need to be crafted for each situation.
- People with financial needs are usually people in pain. Attending to them personally and identifying with their pain may be more important than dealing with financial solutions. People can live with a certain amount of financial discomfort; loneliness, isolation, low self-esteem, and the fear of calamity are far more difficult to bear. Being a caring friend may be more

important than solving financial problems. Channeling people into small groups can be one of the most important methods for sustaining people in crises.

- Offering financial aid to people in financial need is accompanied by the risk of creating dependency. By itself, financial aid is rarely an adequate response to the need.
- The two primary solutions to financial need—decreasing spending and increasing income—almost always require long-term relationships for continued encouragement as new behaviors take root.
- God owns and controls all of the resources of this world. Intercessory prayer can be the most important activity for bringing about change in situations of financial need.

Define the Problem and Identify Abilities

Begin by learning everything you can about the problem, and especially note the person's skills and abilities as they surface in your conversation. Ask yourself, Do I understand the sequence of events or is something missing? If there is something missing, keep asking questions in different ways until you get to the root of the situation. Also ask, Are my questions relevant to the problem? Not all parts of the person's history necessarily pertain to the situation at hand. Being able to explain why you are asking a question is a good test for relevance.

Defining a problem and identifying a person's strengths requires very careful listening. The following techniques will enhance your ability to communicate:

- Ask open-ended questions.
- Ask probing questions: Tell me about …
- Give positive nonverbal messages—lean forward, make eye contact, smile.
- Understand the specific dollar amounts involved in the situation.

Most often you and the individual will define the problem in a similar way. But you may have widely different ideas about the person's ability to deal with the problem and possible steps toward a solution. Remember that the individual has been living through this situation and is likely discouraged about it; you'll need to encourage the individual to rethink the situation based on his or her skills and talents. By the end of this step, you and the person you're helping should agree on a definition of both the problem and the person's abilities to solve the problem.

Consider Options for Solutions

The individual with the need will probably see very few options for dealing with the problem. Most likely he or she has been dealing with the problem for a long time without success. Your fresh outlook will likely enable you to see many more options.

At this point, your task is to help the person identify options based on the abilities you have already helped to identify. Make sure all options are clear and measurable. All should include a role for you and the church. If the individual is unable to express ideas, try naming options that you see in a way that respects the person's past struggles. Be prepared for negative reactions to your options. Help to identify the reasons why those options "won't work."

Encourage dreaming for the future! Don't confine yourself to short-term solutions. Look to where the person wants to be in five or ten years.

Make a Choice

From your point of view, one option will probably stand out as the best, and you will be tempted to make the choice yourself. The individual may even want you to choose for them. *Never* make that choice for the person. He or she *must* make the choice and take responsibility for it. Your task is to accept and validate the person's choice. You'll want to restate the choice several times to be sure of the decision and then begin talking about implementing that choice.

3. Implement a Ministry Plan

Once an option has been chosen, you should develop a plan to implement the solution. The plan should include what the individual will do and what the deacons will do to help the person reach the chosen goals. This stage always includes specific, measurable steps, including a contract, meeting times, and naming any other people who will participate in the process. Use the ministry plan (pp. 38-41) and the budgeting guidelines (pp. 43-45) as a guide for your planning. You will need to commit to following through the ministry plan even if you rotate out of office. Changing players halfway through a plan can derail progress.

4. Follow Up

An integral part of the ministry plan is how you and the church will follow up with the individual. Follow-up meetings, as detailed in the ministry plan, will not be as frequent as during the implementation part of the process, but it is important that you continue to offer support and address continuing issues promptly.

Four Principles for Helpers

1. God gives people energy and skills to solve their own problems and attain their own dreams.
2. Aid produces better and more lasting results when the focus is on helping people solve their own problems instead of temporarily bailing them out.
3. Aid is effective only when it follows comprehensive problem solving.
4. Aid is most effective when it is directed at opportunities rather than problems.

Rebuilding a Life

Try to find how the principles listed above were applied in the following case study.

> Doug, in his late twenties, is married and has two children. When Doug calls the deacons at his church to ask for help with food and housing, they provide enough food to last a week and ask Doug whether he would be open to having a person from the congregation spend some time to help him. Doug agrees. He gets to know Tim, a member of the church who is a gifted listener. The deacons support Tim and stay in touch with him on a monthly basis.

It soon becomes clear that Doug wants to make a new start for himself and his family. His problems include the abuse of drugs and alcohol and irregular work habits. His wife's buying binges further complicate the family's finances.

Tim and the deacons locate a supportive housing situation. They agree to pay the first and last month's rent. Doug agrees to join AA and enroll in a local job-training program. His wife agrees to go for budget counseling.

The job program and the friendship with Tim do wonders for Doug's self-esteem. He finds temporary work while he trains to be a produce manager in a grocery store. Tim regularly invites Doug over to his house to work on projects together.

Things seen to be going well until Doug calls Tim to say that he and his wife, who have a long history of conflict, have split up. Doug is shattered; Tim is at a loss. He shares his frustration with the deacons. Tim meets with a therapist in his congregation and the pastor. They provide some advice and a short list of counselors.

Doug and his wife attend therapy sessions for six months. During this time, Tim meets with Doug once a week to encourage him and help keep him focused. During their conversations Doug talks about "feeling dirty"—he admits that his parents never thought much of him. Tim tells him about God's gift of forgiveness. He urges Doug to join a support group at the church, and Doug hesitantly agrees.

Eventually Doug is able to deal with many of his spiritual struggles. He sometimes comes to church now. He's reading the Bible and some Christian literature on parenting.

Discussion Guide

1. Check In

Take a few minutes for each person to share a reason for thanksgiving and/or an item of concern. Then pray for the person on your right, addressing the concerns expressed by that person.

Read John 4:1-26.

2. On Helpers and Helping

- Review your responses to "A Quiz for Helpers." How did the quiz help put the issue of helping and being helped in perspective?
- Review the section "How Should We Help?" What is the difference between "helping" and "fixing"?
- Review the case study "Going Beyond Relief." How would you respond to Mrs. G's call a month later?

3. Helping People with Financial Needs: A Step-by-Step Guide

- Review the steps presented. Why might the first step, "Time for Reflection," be important?
- Are any of the steps unclear to you?

4. Ministry Plan

- How would the use of a ministry plan help you to work with a family?
- What would you find hardest about using a ministry plan?
- Review the section "Four Principles for Helpers" and the case study that follows it. How are the four principles reflected in this story? Could these principles be helpful in your own work as a deacon?

5. Partners in the Community

Name three or four agencies in the community that your diaconate is involved with. Plan to visit some of them to familiarize yourself with their services.

Don't forget to prepare for the next session by reading "Part 4: Promoting Stewardship and Justice."

1. Check In

Here's another opportunity to build prayer into your session. Ask each person to share a reason for thanksgiving and/or an item of concern. Ask someone to read aloud the suggested Scripture passage, and then highlight the way in which Jesus relates to the woman at the well.

2. On Helpers and Helping

- It's easy for us to take the attitude that we should try to "fix" things. A discussion of your group's responses to the "Quiz for Helpers" and the section "How Should We Help?" should allow you to get at this attitude.
- The example of Mrs. G in the case study "Going Beyond Relief" is not unusual. Often deacons need to choose whether they will simply respond to immediate needs without getting involved in a long-term relationship. Take time especially to discuss how the deacons would respond to the second call. Deacons need to understand that they do not have to help every need that comes their way.

3. Helping People with Financial Needs: A Step-by-Step Guide

Take some time to go through the steps involved in the process. Be sure to go over any that are unclear to your group.

4. Ministry Plan

Take some time to review "Four Principles for Helpers" and the case study "Rebuilding a Life." Identify the ways in which these principles are at work in the case study. Find out whether the deacons in your group agree with these four principles and discuss how the principles might be helpful in carrying out your tasks.

5. Partners in the Community

Take a few minutes to talk with each other about agencies in the community that you as deacons work with. Plan to visit several so that newly elected deacons become familiar with the services these agencies offer.

Ministry Plan

Part 1: Your Mentor

To make major life changes, most people need support from a friend or accountability partner. We call this person a mentor. To the right is the name of the person who has indicated his/her desire to be your mentor. This person has promised to

- pray daily for you.
- meet with you on a weekly basis for at least one hour for support, friendship, and guidance.
- handle any information you share with great care to keep your name and reputation strong.

Deacon: _____

Address: _____

Telephone: _____

Family or individual served: _____

Address: _____

Telephone: _____

Name of Mentor: _____

Address: _____

Telephone: _____

Part 2: Immediate Aid Agreed to and Given

Many people think that the church can make their problems disappear. We cannot do that. Your choices and actions were part of what brought you to this point of need. You must be responsible to solve past problems and create a new future. The purpose of our immediate aid is to help you move past the crisis so that you can take the opportunity to plan and dream about your future. Our aim is not to solve your problems but to partner with you to find creative ways to accomplish your goals.

Date   Describe aid given

_____

_____

_____

_____

_____

_____

_____

_____

_____

Ministry Plan (continued)

Part 3: Goals

As partners, we must first decide what the goal or end result of our work together will be. Our goal must reflect your realistic dream for where you would like to be in the future. Think about these areas of your life: housing, work, education, home life, security, children, spiritual life, friends, income range, skills, and resources. Write down goals that reflect your hopes and dreams for your future. Indicate what kind of time you will need to attain that goal.

1._____

_____

2._____

_____

3._____

_____

4._____

_____

5._____

_____

Part 4: Obstacles

What are some of the problems that keep you from achieving your goals? Using the categories to the right, try to list specific problems that get in the way.

Lack of encouragement or support:

Lack of information:

Lack of skills:

Lack of resources:

Other:

Ministry Plan (continued)

Part 5: Budget

As we go through a simple budgeting process together, we will assess your current situation, plan your budget, and track your progress. This will give you a good picture of your current net worth and current income and spending habits.

Part 6: Special Skills

Although you have needs in certain areas, you can help others with the gifts you have in other areas. List any hobbies, talents, and skills you can use to serve others when needs arise.

Hobbies: _____

Talents: _____

Skills: _____

Part 7: Action Plan

The goal of our partnership is to help you meet your goals. Next we will list steps you can take toward attaining your goals. We will also list what you can count on from us to help meet your goals. Most of the help we give will be other than financial. We will help you access information and the services available to help you meet your goals. Any financial assistance will be directed at helping you create new opportunities for yourself; it will not be directed at problems. Your mentor will pray for you daily and meet with you regularly.

On a separate sheet of paper, write down all the sequential steps necessary to meet each goal. Tell us what you can do to achieve each step, and we will decide what we can do to help.

What will you do to attain your goals?

1._____

2._____

3._____

4._____

5._____

6._____

7._____

8._____

9._____

Ministry Plan (continued)

Note: If you do not fulfill your end of this agreement, we can not fulfill our end of it. If there are good reasons for not following through on this plan, we can renegotiate different goals or steps. Our help is contingent on your taking action for your future.

What will the mentor and deacons do to help?

1._____

2._____

3._____

4._____

5._____

6._____

7._____

8._____

9._____

Part 8: Follow Up

We want to provide all the encouragement, help, and support you need to attain your goals. To do that we need to regularly evaluate whether this is the right plan for you and whether we are on track with it. Most people find that it needs to be amended at various times. It is usually helpful to monitor the plan frequently at first and then less often when all is going according to plan.

Progress in goal attainment will be reviewed
___ Daily   ___ Weekly   ___ Monthly

An overall review and next steps planning process will be held
_____ (month and year).

Other conditions of agreement:

Signed _____ Date_____

Signed _____ Date_____

Assess, Plan, Track

Note: This material is based on the booklet *APT* written by Sherrie Kornoelje of Neighbors Plus, Holland, Michigan. Used by permission. To obtain a copy of the booklet, call 616-399-9190, ext. 103.

Step 1: Assess

The first step in your budgeting process is to assess your current financial picture. By gathering the information you need to take a "snapshot" of your current financial situation, you will be better prepared to make financial goals for your future. Try to update this picture yearly.

Begin by listing your **assets** (everything you own, including cash, property, savings, home, car, investments) and your **liabilities** (everything you owe, including car loans, mortgages, credit card debt, and any other loans). Subtract your total liabilities from your total assets to find your **net worth**. Net worth is the financial total of your life's work to this point. If your net worth isn't what you'd like it to be, do something about it in your plan!

Step 2: Plan

Before putting together your first plan, it's helpful to keep track of all your expenses for a one-month period. To begin your plan, make a list of your monthly **income** and **expenses**. Group your expenses into categories that fit your particular situation. Annual expenses (for example, insurance) should be divided by 12 to indicate your monthly cost. Possible categories include the following:
- giving
- taxes
- savings
- housing
- utilities
- groceries
- dependent care
- transportation

- medical/dental
- insurance
- clothing
- entertainment
- kids

Prepare a ledger sheet for each category with the following headings:

DATE	DESCRIPTION	IN	OUT	BALANCE

After you list all of your monthly income and expenses, add up **total income** and **total expenses.** Your income should be equal to your expenses. If your plan does not balance at zero, you will need to make decisions about increasing income or decreasing expenses (if the balance is negative) or allocating the balance of your income to a long-term category like savings (if the balance is positive). When you have a monthly plan that balances to zero, divide the expenses of your monthly plan into "mini" plans for each pay period. This is the tool you will use each time you receive a paycheck.

Step 3: Track

Your monthly plan is your guide for spending. To make the plan work for you, you need to track your day-to-day spending against the plan.

To begin, divide the current balance of your checking account (or cash) into the categories of your plan. Enter these amounts on the **Balance Forward** line of the ledger sheets (see example below). The total of the Balance Forward line of all the categories should equal the balance of your checking account or your cash on hand.

DATE	GROCERIES	IN	OUT	BALANCE
	Balance Forward			

As you receive income (for example, your paycheck), compare the actual amount to the planned amount. If there is a difference, you'll need to change the plan to accommodate it. Distribute the income of your paycheck into the categories of your mini-plan (see example below). Now you are ready to use your plan for your spending decisions. Whenever you make a purchase, subtract the dollar amount from the appropriate category in your plan. When the balance in that category gets to zero, you need to either stop spending in that area or move money from another category to cover that expense.

DATE	HOUSING	IN	OUT	BALANCE
	Balance Forward			0
1st	Paycheck	257.00		257.00

DATE	CHILD CARE	IN	OUT	BALANCE
	Balance Forward			11.40
1st	Paycheck	80.00		91.40

Here are a few tips to keep in mind:

- Remember to do the tracking as often as possible. An easy way to remember all your purchases is to save your receipts. If you keep your ledger sheets up to date, they will be a valuable tool for making decisions about how much and when to spend.
- Do not write a check from a category without funds. You must decide how you will cover an extra expense and move funds from one category to another. This will help you think through your priorities based on actual needs. Provide a good explanation of the transfer.
- If you are using a cash system, get into the habit of recording the exact amounts of your expenses. For example, if you take $20 to the grocery store and only spend $17.33, put the change back in the envelope and record the exact amount on the ledger.

PART 4

Promoting Stewardship and Justice

Promoting stewardship is an essential part of your calling as a deacon. Stewardship means taking the talents, gifts, and financial resources that God has given us and using them to serve others. The deacons' task is to help the congregation understand that financial stewardship is not simply about "making the budget." Instead, focus on the need of the giver to give. In so doing, you will stimulate God's people to give generously of themselves and link them with opportunities for service.

Deacons are also called to stand up for people who are treated unfairly or oppressed. Once you know about the needs of society's "have-nots," both overseas and in North America, you will want to speak out on their behalf to educate your congregation and partner with them in ministry.

Lead the Congregation into Diaconal Ministry

Each one should use whatever gift he has received to serve others, faithfully administering God's grace in its various forms.

—1 Peter 4:10

It was he who gave some to be apostles, some to be prophets, some to be pastors and teachers, to prepare God's people for works of service, so that the body of Christ may be built up.

—Ephesians 4:11-12

Prompt us [the congregation] to seize new opportunities to worship God with offerings of wealth, time and ability.

—Form for Ordination of Elders and Deacons,
Christian Reformed Church

The special ministries are not an end in themselves.... They function correctly only when they assist the office of all believers to come to its fullest expression."

—Report 44, *Acts of Synod 1973,* p. 693

Church leaders often notice a lack of involvement among members of the congregation. It's easy to assume that lack of involvement is caused by lack of commitment. The lists below identify some of the reasons why people may not be involved, as well as reasons why they do get involved.

Why People May Not Be Involved
- They were never asked.
- They depreciate their gifts.
- They don't know the needs.
- They are afraid they may do it wrong.
- Their past service was not appreciated.
- They're busy in other kingdom work.
- The congregation has not felt its calling to be involved.
- They feel on the "fringe."
- The diaconate is unorganized and fails to communicate.

For Reflection

Which of the reasons listed may be true for the members of your congregation?

Why People Do Get Involved
- They were asked.
- They have identified their gifts.
- They understand the needs.
- They receive training and support.
- Their service is recognized.
- Work is shared; people aren't overloaded.
- The congregation has made an intentional commitment to ministry.
- They feel at home in the church.
- Deacons know how to involve the congregation in service.

Each One, Reach One

The ability of churches and their diaconates to carry out ministry is directly related to the availability of gifted, trained people. The ministry that takes place in a church cannot exceed the breadth and depth of the leadership base.

The term *leadership* goes beyond the pastor and the council. It's essential that officebearers commit themselves to developing leaders within the congregation.

Officebearers Should Equip Others

Common sense tells us that it is unrealistic to expect the pastor, elders, and deacons to provide most of the ongoing preventive care in the church. A congregation works best when it cultivates and utilizes the gifts of its members.

One of the central tasks of the elected leadership in the church is to develop the congregation's ability to provide leadership by serving. Ephesians 4:12-13 states that the purpose of the various offices is "to prepare God's people for works of service." The word *prepare* is sometimes translated as *equip*. This literally means "to put in working order" or "to repair." Your task as a leader is to coach people to maturity so that they can provide leadership in caregiving.

Here are some examples of how this works:

- Deacons encourage those who are good listeners to visit regularly with those who are lonely and shut in.
- The deacons ask people who have the ability to lead small groups to organize a support group for single parents.
- The pastor and the elders set up a network of pastoral care workers in each district of the church to provide some of the ongoing and specialized care. They involve people with the gift of hospitality in leading district meetings.

Draw People into Ministry

The key to developing leaders is to work with apprentices. These are not assistants; they are partners in ministry. In this approach, leaders are always cultivating another person for service. Here are some examples to consider:

- Apprentice a young adult by inviting her along when you gather food for the food bank.
- When delivering food to a single parent in the community, invite someone who is capable of long-term helping ministry.
- When you lead a seminar, ask someone to come along to learn how to do it the next time.

The purpose of this is not to "save time" for the minister or the council members. Instead, you are communicating to God's people that they too can minister effectively and make a vital contribution to the body of Christ as it grows and matures in ministry.

Guidelines for Recruiting

- *Start small, but start.* Build on the motivation and skills of those who have indicated an interest and are willing to help.
- *Offer meaningful opportunities, not just "busy" work.* The opportunity should include some responsibility.
- *Develop diaconal opportunities that challenge and fulfill people.* Create opportunities for growth. Stretch people's ability.
- *Present clear and accurate information about needs, goals, and potential problems.* Tell potential volunteers how much time commitment will be required and what roadblocks or challenges they might find.

Sharon

Sharon, a deacon, is responsible for implementing her church's ministry to single parents. She wants to develop a manual for program volunteers that clearly spells out the program. Sharon knows she doesn't have the time to write it, but she thinks Gail might be interested. Gail, a young mother who was introduced to the church through its single-parent ministry some years earlier, has demonstrated good writing skills.

The next day Sharon invites Gail over for coffee and tells her that she needs help on a project she thinks will interest her. "I know you'll be able to put this together," Sharon says, and goes on to explain her idea. She asks if Gail would be willing to list the activities of all the volunteers

For Reflection

Which of your tasks could you use to recruit others as partners in ministry?

involved in the ministry and describe the process they developed. Together Sharon and Gail brainstorm, write, and laugh. One week later, Gail has the preliminary draft ready. Some revisions and additions later, Sharon presents the finished manual to the deacons.

Bill

Bill is the deacon responsible for working with a community agency that collects and sends gently used clothing to people in need. He's been asked to line up some volunteers from the congregation for some specific projects. During coffee time after church, he notices George standing by himself. "Say, George, sorry to take up your time," says Bill. "I know you've got lots of important things to do. But—well, I know you probably won't be interested—but the deacons delegated me to ask you to help out in a simple little job.

"See, we've got a bunch of used clothing, and it needs to be sorted and stacked before we ship it. It's kind of a pain, I guess, but after all it is a project the whole church approved ... and it's a real simple job. Any fool could do it. And it would only take a few moments one evening. What do you say? Will you do it? You're not going to let me down, are you? After all, this is Kingdom work, you know!"

Ken

Ken is one of the deacons who is working with a family with financial problems. He approaches a member of the congregation with a specific skill that may enable him to help. "Jonathan, the deacons have run into a problem we think you might be able to help us with. We're working with a family that's having a lot of trouble paying its bills. One of the main causes, as I see it, is that they live in a house that does not hold any heat. Their utility bills are sky high, and they can't afford to have a contractor look into it.

"You know a lot about heating and insulation. I wonder if you would come with me to visit this family next week to see what you think and what advice you might have. I'd like to help this family stave off bankruptcy, and that is what might happen unless we do something. Would you be available?"

For Reflection

How were the guidelines for recruiting used (or not used!) in the examples of Sharon, Bill, and Ken?

Grow in the Grace of Giving

The financial statements for last year are in and the news is not great. Once again there is a shortfall in the church's budget. In addition, the amount the church pays to support the denomination's ministries (called ministry shares) has fallen to 68 percent of the church's commitment.

This happened despite some last-minute pleas from the council in November urging the congregation to make one last push to make the budget. Even though it was Advent, the pastor was persuaded to include the subject of giving in one of his sermons!

There is vigorous discussion around the council table. Finally, someone makes the motion to ask the deacons to come up with a plan for the coming year.

This church's approach to stewardship and giving is focused on the budget and the shortfall. It also assumes that one group in the church is responsible for "fixing" it.

Focus on the Need of the Giver to Give

A church's approach to stewardship and giving must begin from the need of the giver to give; not the need of the church to receive. Giving is a part of our sanctification. It reflects our spiritual walk with God. And just as we need to grow in our faith, our conduct, and our insight, we need to "excel in this grace of giving" (2 Cor. 8:7).

Helping people in the church to grow in the grace of giving is not the same as "meeting the budget." Think of the budget as a planning tool. It inspires no one and certainly does not motivate anyone to give. That is why it is so puzzling that most churches have offerings for the church's budget. We don't pay for "the budget"; we give so that ministry can happen.

A study of giving patterns in many churches reveals that most people still give the same amount as they did two years ago. That isn't necessarily because they are on a fixed income.

A church budget can actually limit a person's giving. After all, one may wonder, if the church made out fine with the amount I gave last year, why change? Shifting the focus to the need for the giver to grow instead of what the church needs to receive brings about a dramatic shift of perspective.

Give Like the Macedonians

You can help people discover the joy of giving if you see it as a faith response. Most people tend to emphasize giving as a burden, a sacrifice, a duty, a commitment. Second Corinthians 8 and 9 paint a different picture—a picture of people who experienced "overflowing joy" in their giving, even though they were extremely poor. These passages contain a number of biblical principles about giving. Our giving is to be

- regular (on the first day of the week)
- firstfruits (not leftovers)
- proportional (as we have been blessed)
- cheerful (without compulsion)
- generous (expecting a blessing)
- sacrificial (beyond expectations)

Stewardship Committee

Pastor Elders Deacons

Who Should Take the Lead?

Let's go back to the discussion of the budget shortfall. Remember how it ended? The council gave it to the deacons to prepare a plan. They were right in thinking that someone has to prepare a plan. And we've already noted that deacons are responsible for promoting stewardship.

But it's important to realize that stewardship is a *shared* responsibility. One way to picture this is as a three-legged stool supported by elders, deacons, and the pastor. In this model each partner has a role to play, and a stewardship committee coordinates their efforts.

The *pastor* can preach and teach about the biblical principles and the joy of giving. *Elders* need to affirm people in their giving and encourage them to grow in this area as a part of their sanctification. *Deacons* can inform the congregation about the ministries they support, teach biblical stewardship, and inspire people to dedicate themselves and their gifts and resources to the Lord. A *stewardship committee* can coordinate these efforts and develop a plan for an annual focus on stewardship. Your denominational office is a good place to check for resources about stewardship.

Stewardship Is a "Whole Life" Commitment

Giving financially is only a part of our stewardship response to God. The stewardship of our time and talents includes the call to offer ourselves to God as a living sacrifice (Rom. 12:1).

Again, the focus is not on the need of the church to receive those gifts, but on the need of the congregation to grow in service. Every church needs a systematic way of helping people discover their gifts and placing them in fruitful service. You'll find that people who are involved in ministry according to their gifts usually give more financially—each part of stewardship reinforces the others.

The stewardship of creation is also part of our "whole life" commitment. Seeing ourselves as stewards, not owners, of the world we live in makes a major difference in our spiritual attitude towards our possessions.

Stewardship is our response of gratitude to God's grace. It is part of our sanctification. To nurture this gratitude, deacons need to encourage a whole-life commitment to being good stewards. Then we will (re)discover the joy of giving.

Six Initiatives to Encourage Growth in Giving

As your church develops a program to encourage stewardship and joyful giving, you may find it helpful to explore a variety of approaches. Here are six initiatives, drawn from a variety of sources, to consider. They are written up in the form of proposals for your church. Try each one for size. After you read each initiative, answer the following questions:

- What do I like about this initiative?
- How could we adapt this for use in our church?

1. Preach and Teach About Stewardship and Giving

- Our pastor and every member of council will personally and prayerfully review their personal giving patterns and view of money. We as leaders will model "the grace of giving."
- Our pastor will preach two to four times per year about the biblical teachings on stewardship, the principles of giving, and the joy of giving.
- Our church will sponsor seminars on financial stewardship, estate planning, and budgeting. The goal is to reach a variety of audiences.
- Our bulletins will contain regular inserts about stewardship. We will highlight the practical implications of biblical teaching in these inserts.
- Our church education program will make creative use of existing resources (from denominational and local ministries) to teach stewardship to our children.

2. Dedicate the Offering

- Our worship service will highlight the offering time as an act of worship, not simply a time to collect money and take a break.
- The deacons (or a representative) will offer a prayer of dedication after each offering.
- Deacons will use creative means to show the congregation that the offering is a time of dedication to the Lord.
- We will clearly explain the ministry being carried out by each of the offerings we gather. This may include any of the following:
  —a booklet explaining the ministries of the church
  —stories about the ministry's impact
  —sharing the ministry's needs, blessings, and prayer requests

3. Increase Ministry Opportunities

- Our pastor, the deacons, the elders, and other leaders will find creative ways to involve each member of our congregation in a ministry where they make a difference in the life of another person.
- Deacons will vigorously promote service opportunities in the community and around the world, especially in ministries we support financially.
- Young people will be given specific opportunities for service to the church and to the community.
- We will regularly invite people to share the challenges and blessings of their personal experience in ministry.
- Our congregation will be involved in missions. We will support missionaries and encourage members of the congregation to serve on a mission field.

4. Invite a Firstfruits Response

- We will invite members of the church to prayerfully review their approach to giving to ensure that each is giving "first to God" as a thank offering.
- In their home visits, elders will encourage members of the church to regularly examine their giving patterns and to grow in giving.
- Members of the church will be invited to complete the "Grow One" challenge (see p. 54) as an opportunity to intentionally grow in our giving.

The "Grow One" Challenge

1. From the left-hand column find the appropriate figure representing the approximate annual income for your family.
2. Move your eyes to the right until you find the amount closest to your weekly giving level (annual commitment divided by 52).
   Enter that number: $_____.
3. Move your eyes to the top of the chart to determine what percentage that is of your income.
4. Move one (or more) column to the left to consider "growing one" and move your eyes back down to your original weekly giving line to see what your new weekly commitment would be.
   Enter that number: $_____.
5. Subtract the amount you wrote for #2 from the amount you wrote for #4: $_____. This is the amount of your weekly increase to "grow one" in financial commitment while growing many steps in your faith relationship with God.

Weekly Giving Chart

INCOME	15%	12%	10%	9%	8%	7%	6%	5%	4%	3%	2%	1%
5,000	14	12	10	9	8	7	6	5	4	3	2	1
10,000	29	23	19	17	15	13	12	10	8	6	4	2
15,000	43	35	29	26	23	20	17	14	12	9	6	3
20,000	58	46	38	35	31	27	23	19	15	12	8	4
25,000	72	58	48	43	38	34	29	24	19	14	10	5
30,000	87	69	58	52	46	40	35	29	23	17	12	6
35,000	101	81	67	61	54	47	40	34	27	20	13	7
40,000	115	92	77	69	62	54	46	38	31	23	15	8
45,000	130	104	87	78	69	61	52	43	35	26	17	9
50,000	144	115	96	87	77	67	58	48	38	29	19	10
55,000	159	127	106	95	85	74	63	53	42	32	21	11
60,000	173	138	115	104	92	81	69	58	46	35	23	12
65,000	188	150	125	113	100	88	75	63	50	38	25	13
70,000	202	162	135	121	108	94	81	67	54	40	27	13
75,000	216	173	144	130	115	101	87	72	58	43	29	14
80,000	231	185	154	138	123	108	92	77	62	46	31	15
85,000	245	196	163	147	131	114	98	82	65	49	33	16
90,000	260	208	173	156	138	121	104	87	69	52	35	17
95,000	274	219	183	164	146	128	110	91	73	55	37	18
100,000	288	231	192	173	154	135	115	96	77	58	38	19

5. Annual Stewardship Month
- Each year, our stewardship committee will plan and carry out a stewardship month which will include
  —bulletin inserts for three or four Sundays
  —a sermon or two
  —an invitation to grow one step in giving
- Each year we will build on the experience of the previous one; growing one step in our creativity and boldness!

6. Estimate of Giving Card
- We will encourage our members to fill in an "estimate of giving" card as part of their response to stewardship month. These cards will be gathered during a worship service as part of our offering to the Lord.
- People who attend a preconfession class or a premarital counseling session will intentionally explore the biblical principles of stewardship and learn to plan firstfruits giving.

The Offering as an Act of Worship

Consider these suggestions for making the offering a meaningful part of your church's worship. Perhaps the deacons could explore these with your church's worship committee.

Tell a Story

Introduce the offering by telling a story about someone who has been helped by this ministry. Explain what the organization hopes to do with the money. Telling how one person has been helped brings the ministry to life and provides an opportunity to express appreciation for the prayers and gifts of God's people.

If someone in your congregation works for the organization, let that person tell a story. Be clear about time limits and what you want. If not, let the deacons tell the story of how the ministry will make a difference.

Pray Specifically

Before or after the offering pray for the organization's ministry. Be specific. Some agencies put out prayer calendars with specific requests. If you don't know what to pray for, call the organization the week before and ask,
- What specific needs can we pray for?
- Are you facing a particular challenge that we could pray for?

Involve the Children

Here are some suggestions for giving children meaningful opportunities to participate in worship. Be sure to avoid any sense that they are performing for the congregation.
- Every time you have a food drive, ask two children to bring up a small basket of food and place it next to the offering.

- Ask the church school children to come up to the front for a children's message. Explain where the money they have collected in church school will go, and give the money to one of the deacons.
- Invite the young people to gather the offering. Be sure to provide specific instructions.

Use Music to Highlight a Cause

Involve children, your church youth group, or a church choir in the offering by having them sing hymns or choruses whose themes highlight the cause of an offering on a particular Sunday. There are hymns that speak eloquently about causes like hunger, homelessness, or Christian education. Music is a worshipful way of allowing us to celebrate the importance and meaning of participating in such forms of ministry. If your offering is for an overseas ministry, choose music from that particular country to highlight the cause.

Act on It!

Have a number of people from the worship committee or youth group plan a short drama or role play that demonstrates how the offering will make a difference in people's lives. This can be especially effective in a special service like Thanksgiving.

Also appropriate at Thanksgiving is an offering of symbols of people's work. Ask representatives of various careers to come forward to share how God uses them in those areas.

Reverse the Offering

A reverse offering is a great way to gather specific items of food, clothing, or other items needed by an agency. Prepare slips of paper with the names of the items on them, one item per slip. Explain to the congregation that they are welcome to take one or more slips. Ask them to bring those items to a designated place the following Sunday.

Celebrate the Budget

Prepare a booklet for your congregation that focuses on ministries that are possible because of budget contributions.

Be Prophetic Critics

The form for ordination we've already quoted saves one of its best lines for last: "Be prophetic critics of the waste, injustice, and selfishness in our society, and be sensitive counselors to the victims of such evils." That too is the calling of deacons.

Some deacons prefer to pick up on the last part of that line and work as counselors with "victims of such evils." But the simple truth is that most people who are treated unjustly will often continue to be treated this way, no matter how much we help them cope.

Think of a single mother who can't get quality housing for herself and her two children. Although she may be helped in the short term with additional financial support in order to secure better quality housing, we need to ask, Who will walk

56

with her the next time she needs affordable housing?

In this situation, it would be more helpful if a deacon were to accompany her on the house hunt and remind landlords that they are not allowed to discriminate when they rents out their units. If a landlord does so, you as a deacon representing your church will take your concerns about this landlord to the authorities.

"Give a Man a Fish …"

We've already mentioned the importance of "teaching a person to fish" rather than simply "giving a fish." But there's more to this metaphor. It does not help to teach a person to fish if he or she does not have access to good fishing spots. That kind of access is a matter of justice. Deacons are called to advocate for justice for those in need.

For example, refugees caught in the middle of civil strife need an opportunity to make a fresh start in another country, often through sponsorship by a church or family. Until recently, when refugees came to Canada, they were charged a "head tax" of $975 per person to come into the country. That is money a refugee does not have. Churches, the community that has sponsored so many refugees, advocated for several years for the removal of this tax. Recently that tax was removed for refugees but is still in place for immigrants. So our work is not done.

Jubilee for Today

The Bible offers several examples of how God cares about the poor. The year of Jubilee is one such way. God decreed that every fiftieth year people's debts were to be canceled.

This principle has recently received a twenty-first century application in a campaign called Jubilee 2000. Jubilee 2000 calls for the cancellation of debts owed by the poorest countries of the world. The Canadian government announced it would cancel all of the debt owed by Bangladesh, and the Prime Minister is committed to canceling all of the debts owed to Canada by poor countries. The United States Congress is considering several bills aimed at debt relief for poor countries.

Think Globally, Act Locally

Being part of a global campaign may not be the place you want to begin as a new deacon. But you can begin to work for justice right in your own community.

Think back to the case study of Susan (Part 2). In that situation, deacons could
- advocate with her to make sure that her husband pays the adequate child support and that he pays it on a monthly basis.
- help her get access to affordable housing.
- make sure she has access to quality daycare so that she can support her family.

Advocating with people does not mean speaking for them. We walk alongside people in need so that they can find their own voice. Our task is to echo and amplify that voice.

As you work for justice for those who experience the pain of injustice, treat them as coworkers. They are "victims" only in the sense that they do not deserve to be treated in this way, not in the sense that they are powerless to act.

Being a prophetic critic means you will have to challenge some people and groups to act differently. They will not always thank you. Some might even tell you to stick to doing works of mercy. Remind them that the best way to show mercy and walk humbly with God is to "do justice."

Doing justice is one way God gives us to love our neighbor and our God. "What does the LORD require of you? To act justly and to love mercy and to walk humbly with your God" (Micah 6:8). That is your awesome challenge as deacons. With God's help you can carry out the task.

Discussion Guide

1. Check In
- Take a few minutes to talk about your calling as a deacon. What excites you about it? What concerns or questions do you have?
- Pray for God to lead you and equip you in your calling.
- Read Ephesians 4:12-13; 2 Corinthians 8:1-5.

2. Reach Out and Recruit
Review the sections "Each One Reach One" and "Guidelines for Recruiting." Then make a list of some of your main tasks as a deacon:

1._____
2._____
3._____
4._____
5._____

- Think of some ways to get people in the congregation involved in that work.
- How would you go about recruiting someone to help with these tasks?

3. Grow in the Grace of Giving
- Who is responsible for developing a stewardship program in your church? Who should be?
- Which of the six initiatives ("Six Initiatives to Encourage Growth in Giving") would be helpful in your church?
- Which of the suggestions in the section "The Offering as an Act of Worship" would be worth trying in your church?

4. Be Prophetic Critics
- Why is it important to "do justice" when you work with others?

5. Wrap Up
- What was especially helpful to you in this time of orientation? What could be improved?
- What would you like to spend more time on in the coming months?
- What else do you need to learn in order to be an effective deacon?

Leaders

1. Check In

This final session is a good time to discuss what excites people about being a deacon and what concerns they may have. Lead the group in a time of prayer for God's leading. Read (or ask someone else to read) the Scripture passages, which particularly point to stewardship of people's gifts and finances. Stress the theme of equipping people to serve so that they may experience joy in their giving.

2. Reach Out and Recruit

The emphasis in the sections "Each One, Reach One" and "Guidelines for Recruiting" is on finding ways to involve the congregation in your work as deacons. Look over the list of tasks you filled in for the discussion guide and discuss how deacons involve members of the congregation in that work. Share ideas for effective recruiting from the examples given.

3. Grow in the Grace of Giving

The readings for this section are quite extensive. The goal should be to get new deacons to start thinking about this topic. Begin the conversation by asking the questions in the discussion guide.

4. Be Prophetic Critics

This section will help your group to understand that justice is part of your work as deacons, especially in working locally.

5. Wrap Up

Take a few minutes to encourage feedback about these orientation sessions. Ask deacons for suggestions on how to improve it. Use the questions in the discussion guide (or your own) to discuss the orientation and to begin thinking about what comes next.

Resources

- *Faith and Finances: Helping People Manage Their Money.* Copublished by CRC Publications and MidAmerica Leadership Foundation. 1-800-333-8300.

  A tool for educating individuals in your congregation and community about wise financial management. Topics include stewardship, the relationship between faith and values, and the steps to financial security.

- *Firstfruits: Managing the Master's Money.* The Barnabas Foundation. Available from CRC Publications. 1-800-333-8300.

  This course examines the whys and hows of stewardship and leads groups to take a closer look at their own relationships with money and things.

- Heerspink, Robert C. *Becoming a Firstfruits Congregation: A Stewardship Guide for Church Leaders.* Grand Rapids, Mich.: CRC Publications. 1-800-333-8300.

  Churches that want to develop a stewardship program would do well to begin with this self-directed study guide. For councils and small group study.

- *The Idea Book: The Best of Firstfruits.* The Barnabas Foundation. Available from CRC Publications. 1-800-333-8300.

  Examples of materials that have been helpful in many churches.

- *The Joy of Giving.* Grand Rapids, Mich.: CRC Publications. 1-800-333-8300.

  A guide to helping congregations understand the biblical teachings on stewardship. Includes worship planning guide for three services, a devotional guide for members of the congregation, and session plans for a church education unit on stewardship for children through adults.

- Miller, Herb. *The Consecration Sunday Stewardship Program.* Nashville: Cokesbury. 1-800-672-1789.

  A simple, easy-to-use way to encourage people to grow one step in their giving.

- Vandezande, Ben. *Developing a Workplan in Your Diaconate*. Diaconal Ministries in Eastern Canada. Available from CRC Publications. 1-800-333-8300.

  Will help your diaconate identify its purpose and develop a work plan. Emphasizes placing deacons in areas of ministry where they are gifted and getting the congregation involved. Includes four half-hour sessions you can do in your diaconate.

- Van Groningen, Jay. *Changing Times, New Approaches*. Grand Rapids, Mich.: CRC Publications. 1-800-333-8300.

  An excellent next step in your development as a deacon. Will equip deacons with new ideas for defining their work, developing their vision, working with needy families, and more.

- Vincent, Mark. *A Christian View of Money*. Waterloo, Ont: Herald Press. 1-519-747-5722.

  Zeroes in on the biblical teaching of money. Mentions seven initiatives a congregation can take to encourage giving.